Also by Lynn McGee

Bonanza
Heirloom Bulldog

Sober Cooking

Poems by Lynn McGee

SPUYTEN DUYVIL
New York City

Cover design by Robert Gizis, based on the 15-foot, outdoor steel sculpture *Fish Tree* by Tobias Flores and Zbigniew Ben Pingot, on permanent display at the Unified Port of San Diego sculpture garden. Cover title design and typography by Maggie Cousins.

©2016 Lynn McGee
ISBN 978-1-941550-51-9

Library of Congress Cataloging-in-Publication Data

McGee, Lynn.
[Poems. Selections]
Sober Cooking / Lynn McGee.
pages cm
ISBN 978-1-941550-51-9
I. Title.
PS3613.C4574A6 2015
811'.6--dc23
2015007038

Dedicated to Robbie (Roberta) Mueller
and in memory of Pamela McGee Davis (1956-1999)
and Bill McGee (1930-2014)

Contents

Root   1

I. Small Flame

Scar   5
Our First ER   6
Prey   8
ER 2   9
Small Flame   10
West Village Sidewalk Café   12
Written in the Sky   14

II. When to Look, or Look Away

Lilies   17
Cold Star   18
Let Me Pass   19
Flight Path   21
Fall   22
I Leave You Listed   23
Deli Night   24
Together   25
Upstairs   26
Celebrating Your Birthday   27

III. A Beautiful, Salvaged Form

Pocket of Life   31
Incoming Call   32
A Noisy Silence   33
Dumpster Love   34
Daily Life   35
The In-Between   36

Sober Laundry	37
The List	38
This Is It	40
Frankenstein, My Love	42
Night	43

IV. A Space Carved Clean

Light	47
Promise	48
Even Now, I Look For You	49
Green	50
What My Neighbors Taught Me	51
Moving On	52
Mars	53
Pinkish Hue	54
Dinner Date	55
After Hearing Your Message	56
Lunch, After Time Apart	57
The Usefulness of Storms	58

V. Burnt Scent Rising

Discovery	61
Hawai'i	62
Sparks	63
Hers	64
Biking at the End of Summer	65
We Climb to an Empty Roof	66

VI. Beveled Edge Shining

Comfort Food	69
Dog	70
Nest	71
Mother, Sister, Friend	73
Flight	74
Sober Cooking	75
Killing Time at the Cubby Hole	77
The Dead Visit Before a Routine Procedure	79
Urban Renewal	80
Acknowledgements	83
Notes	85

Root

Rifling through the deep bin of ginger root,
I find one that is both plump and gnarled,
heavy with moisture
and gleaming, slick when sliced.

How long will I see your absence,
in the small steps of my life?

I.
SMALL FLAME

Scar

Sometimes I see your scar,
dark track where your breast
once was. I see you kneeling,
that first time in my bed,
sinewy arms pulling
the black muscle T-shirt
over your head.
I see your surprised smile
as I pull out a tiny bottle,
squeeze a glistening bead
onto your fingers—
*I'm giving you all kinds
of permission*—and I feel
that tender rush, as you
slow us down.

Our First ER

I saw your red jacket
before I saw you, kicking
through snow
on the train platform,
picking me up that first weekend
I stayed at your house.
I hadn't had breakfast,
and you stood at the stove
flipping *plantanos*,
your lanky frame turned sideways
toward the table where I sat
holding a hot mug,
breathing nutmeg and steam.
It snowed that afternoon,
and into the night.
The muffled scrape of shovels
started early,
and I woke with a stab
when I inhaled,
so you drove us to the ER,
carried my backpack,
scolded the staff for giving me
two bracelets—each
with a different name—
then quietly,
in the harsh light,
asked permission to guard
my care, and I said *Yes*.

I pulled a sweater
over the stiff blue gown.
You pulled the rattling curtain
around my bed and invited
a nurse with long braids
to witness our vows
as you sign the health proxy
and pass it to me.

Prey

The skull of a small child waited
two million years
before some scientist puzzled
over gouges in its surface,
signature etched
into brittle plates
by a flying
raptor's talons.

Hitchcock understood that terror,
something swooping down to skewer
and carry us off,
Cary Grant sprinting
across a cornfield, twisting
to look over his shoulder,
crop duster screaming, wheels
down, poised to grab—

and who hasn't raced
across that field, felt that shadow,
life about to change in ways
that wrench us
from the ballasts we've relied on,
or imagined were there.

ER 2

You fell, and science
caught you.
A nest of tubes
caught you.
Strings of red and blue lights
caught you,
the signature of your heart peaked
and dipped,
and you sent me a message:
love, in familiar words,
then *Substitute this,*
for any affirmation.

Small Flame

The stroke team, fierce as aliens
in their masks and harsh lights,
rolled you back to your room,
sitting high in your bed and flashing
a victory smile,
bag of magic dripping
into your veins, danger dissolving
like falling stars.

My hero, you called out to the neurologist,
Close call, he chimed in,
tapping your feet. *Lift your right arm—No,
your other right arm*,
his face going stern when you couldn't
say your name—then time
slowed.
The room cleared. Your mother
arrived, a furious crow, yelling
down the hall at me, *Go home!
You're not family! Go home!*
and you twisted your face,
a curtain away.

That night I sat by your bed,
repeating, *Your body is already
remembering itself*,
and you shook your head, *No*,
finally mouthing, *I'll try*,
as light reflected off the East River,
saturating the room.

And you did try, and got back
your words, and your sardonic eyebrow,
and pressed your feet
against the therapist's hands.
Friends spoon-fed you cranberry juice
and crushed ice.
Your narrow body cramped,
and you gripped my hand
as the clock moved its heavy arms.

Then surgeons took over,
and sewed a pump into your chest.
A machine forced your breath
and they closed ranks around you.

I see you at the stove, stirring black beans
and corn, hands fragrant with basil.

I see your son—feet big, arms wild—clattering
down the stairs, to hug me goodbye.

I see you smiling in your old way,
tubes rooted in your arm: *Life's too short
for bullshit. Get the spare parts
and fix me*—and I hold
like a small flame, your face
against white pillows.

West Village Sidewalk Café

An ant trail of pedestrians streams
down the block and my table
rocks, making the rainbow
from a sun-speared
glass of white wine, twitch.
The waitress
has shaved her head,
and fans me with lashes thick
as awnings.
The UPS guy's dreadlocks
fill a snood that bounces
as he heads back to his truck.
Happy Hour prices,
I just learned, are inside only,
and two young women resembling
my nieces—swooping hair,
bodies shrink-wrapped
in color—appreciate
the heads-up.
I'm the only customer
beneath these giant,
green umbrellas.
I'm the only person banned
from my lover's room at Weill
Cornell, forbidden near its monitors,
pumps and swinging bags of fluid,
her mother waving a wand
that erased me, statue of sand
hit by wind.

Grating on the sidewalk rattles;
a train tunnels past.
People text and walk,
and look up, wincing.
I am translucent, a ghost
with a wallet,
but I sign the receipt
in my quick way,
awakened by my name.

Written in the Sky

There's no surface my species won't
carve into, no living thing
we won't alter, drain, erase. *We don't
make the water,* we make the water
rancid. *We don't make
the forest,* we make the forest fall.
Feed your animals first,
my grandfather advised,
and I heard, *Give as you take,
or starve us all.*
What would he make
of this life, feeding only myself,
leaning on the railing
of my balcony,
holding with two hands, a triangle
of watermelon tricked
into seedlessness? I hear a buzz
and look up;
a small plane veers,
letters feather against blue sky
in a word I can't read.
I want to fix everything,
and start over. I say, *Sweetheart,
come home,* but I'm speaking
to a ghost.

II.

When to Look, Or Look Away

Lilies

Anger is a dry branch, quick to snap,
but love clouds the air like pollen.

I could shower you in its pastel weight.
It's spring and I've had plenty of time
to let you fade, yet there you are,

shaking the silver colander
under the faucet,
dropping sections of the *Times*
like molted petals
all around you, on the couch.

The lilies along the fence
must be blooming by now,
blossoms gaping, yellow residue
coating their stamens, aroma
vexing you,
I remember, spreading
their confusion
of beauty and death.

Cold Star

1.
The night before I moved out,
we slept in our bed
and the windows, stripped of curtains,
blinked with each passing car.
Some time in the night, I drifted,
crowding you toward the mattress edge,
and when you mildly pushed that place
where my back curves to meet
the open claw of ribs,
I woke myself with zero-to-sixty,
heaving sobs. You slid your arm
around me till the noise stopped,
and neither of us spoke.

2.
I don't want you to think I don't miss you,
you wrote. *I go looking
for you in my sleep, and wake
when I don't find you.*

3.
I am a cold star opening in a new bed.
Blankets slow my turns
till I curl into what feels like my place,
waking in the night because it shifted,
and finding it again.

Let Me Pass

I'm wearing headphones,
Sonny Rollins' bouncy tenor sax
and cymbal line vying
to cheer me up,
windows flashing with each lantern
imbedded in the tunnels'
charred sides.
A few passengers are asleep,
riding jolts of the train
with an easy grace the rest of us lose
in our resistance to lurching,
stations on my new route
becoming familiar—
Bergen, Nevins, Clark.

Last weekend, three men folded blankets
and swung dollies into a truck.
They heaved down my sofa cocooned
in plastic,
gently lowered my bicycle
like a beauty queen
from her float.
Watching from a balcony,
suddenly mine, I tracked
the moving truck's long, white roof
gliding down the block,
and turned to face boxes packed
in a dining room where I had long been
absent at the table,

momentum still in play this morning
as the subway slows
and I jam papers into my backpack,
rising as if for an urgent task—
Excuse me. Excuse me.
Let me pass.

Flight Path

My new apartment faces jets
heading inbound,
their flight path an arrow aimed down
at Brooklyn,
plateauing over black tar roofs
and wooden water towers—giant
belted kegs on spindly legs.

Every minute or so, a blinking light
appears. It hovers, expands,
descends.
The jets find me,
in my gold arm chair angled
toward the windows.
The spectacular star appears,
and my fear, a jagged, creaking ship
loosens from its moorings,
is pulled piece by piece
into the cold sky.

Fall

This is where I fell on ice—
right here, where the sidewalk dips,
and a woman who walks her grandson to pre-K
stopped to help me up. I thanked her
and thanked her,
but wanted you, and held my bloody palm
all day, like an offering.

Now the heel of my hand shines,
where the wound knitted shut.
A pyramid of trash bags rattles
at the curb.
Heat surges from a chimney
across the street, and a distant highrise
trembles in the wavy air.
Sometimes I run into the woman
who helped me when I fell,
and we laugh like old friends—
I'm showing off
how far I've come, how untouched
I am, by all that's passed,
and we're howling
at her grandson's truculent
dragging of feet, his knowing glare.

I Leave You Listed

I leave you listed as my partner
on Facebook
for the same reason you keep
Dusty's cone-shaped collar
from the vet's in your attic,
white plastic gaping
on the floor near a shaft of light,
dust motes swimming
toward heaven.
It isn't that I'm lying about you,
as much as lying
about that dream I still fold myself
into—and you, I think, still love
the gentle race dog
hobbling on three legs,
still miss being
her protector, the one who
makes things right.

Deli Night

A cop writes on her narrow pad,
revolver jutting from its holster,
and the man at the register nods in relief
at whatever she's saying.
I heave a half-gallon of milk
up to the counter,
and he stretches down with my change,
able to see, from his platform,
all three aisles as well as fish-eye mirrors
at every corner.
Most nights, he stands like a sentry,
cigarette behind his ear,
and talks to the old man crouched on a crate
by the open door,
both of them going quiet when a car
with darkened windows, speakers
throbbing, pauses at the curb.
They arm themselves with nonchalance.
The men at the deli know when
to look, and when
to look away, and if I choose
less wisely, I have only
myself to blame.

Together

Seagulls land on the rusty spine
of a tin roof,
fan their wings and nibble
translucent quills.
Steam tumbles from a smokestack,
wraps the birds as if excited
by their industrious grooming,
and they alight and fly as one;
close, but maintaining
alignment,
skillful as commuters exiting
the subway's crowded stairway—
left leg rising behind left leg,
right behind right—climbing
toward sun.
I admire that march,
and the flock's daring maneuvers,
how living things manage
the delicate cohesion
that moves them
as one, and gets them
where they want.

Upstairs

Eventually, I begin to gather myself up,
old selves and new,
and come across you standing
in our room,
adjusting the music's volume
like a low flame on the stove,
lighting candles, bowing over cinnamon
and vanilla, your shoulders
brown from kneeling in the garden,
left hand clicking the lighter
till each wick is caught.
I see myself too, in that room,
sitting up in bed watching,
and I not only feel
what my earlier self is feeling,
I become her again,
someone to rush upstairs for,
at day's end, and surround
with beauty.

Celebrating Your Birthday

The calendar triggers a memory,
how I tried to stay awake
after we made love in our warm
bed, and as I resisted
the pull of sleep, I'd blurt out
nonsense:
Am I on the right train?
waking myself long enough to hear:
You're right here with me,
where you belong,
and then it would be morning.
Happy Birthday,
my memory. Happy Birthday
to you.

III.

A Beautiful, Salvaged Form

Pocket of Life

I stayed in all weekend,
listening to American soul from the days
when lovers ground shag carpets flat
with their bodies.
I wore headphones and ate carrots,
chewing loud as a Sauropod grazing
beneath a comet-streaked sky.
I had another glass of wine
and channel surfed a while,
napped in the soaring canopy
of a redwood forest, rocked in a cage
of branches and rotting leaves,
salamanders dropped by hawks
and writhing in the soggy bed
of new soil,
hundreds of generations
never setting foot on the ground
far below,
or knowing they were trapped
in a pocket of life.

Incoming Call

After the hand-scrawled sign,
Family Only,
that blocked me
from your room,
after I paced outside
your life, a starving wolf,
lair avalanched shut,
after winter,
then spring,
you called me one night,
and we spoke
screen to small screen.
The voice you'd lost
and found
was slower,
but I drank the sound of it
and asked you to angle
the phone
so I could see
your sleeping hand,
the arm that would
never wake,
the outline of long legs
that my legs remember,
so I could say good-bye,
in my way,
to all the parts of you.

A Noisy Silence

A phalanx of men in Spandex shorts
races past me on wafer-thin bikes,
takes a corner
with synchronized flare,
school of tropical fish.

I can't match their speed,
but make a point of defying
a speed bump,
lift my ass slightly, as if jumping
a horse,
and another biker, boxers rising
above his pants, cuts
in front of me,
shoots through the red light.

You're living the wrong life,
some old voice scolds,
and I shift gears to maximize speed
on the downhill,
wind drowning out the music
on my headphones, making
a noisy silence.

Dumpster Love

He was leaning back against
a dumpster; chin up,
eyes closed when I biked past,

and she stood facing him,
hand inside his open zipper,
right arm a piston,
feet planted as if braced
on a ship's tilting deck.

Their storm made her pleated
skirt dance. A little girl
stood watching,
then wrested her pink bike
in the opposite direction

and glided beside me as we
distanced ourselves
from the vigorous
exchange—which surely
she knew wasn't love,
though it commanded our exit,
sent a blaring proclamation
that no space
is inviolate, and if you
don't agree, leave.

Daily Life

If you were still in my life, you'd know
Franklin Avenue smells like burning rubber
and the motorcycle club on the corner
asserts dominion,
searing the air with fierce revving
and fitful combustion.
You'd know the Mister Softee jingle
has been waking me,
relentless
as a horror film—empty street,
then close-up on the driver's
maniacal glee.
Maybe he was the one,
selling meth from his truck.
Maybe he was cruising my block
with its towering construction,
elevators reeking of weed,
my neighbors careening down
the sidewalk,
shedding discretionary income
sweet as pheromones.
Who wouldn't want a piece of that?
And that's where you'd stop me,
if you were still in my life,
and we'd go back and forth
in our easy way, and it wouldn't
matter, about what.

The In-between

Given what's gone down—all night vigils
at the hospital, the gut-punch
of loss—*The Sopranos*
was not the best choice on cable
tonight, and I've muted Tony
on a ventilator to stare
at the refrigerator, idling like a bus.

I'm joined on the couch by a cat—waves
of lava fur, and a hair-trigger response
to noise. She'll take that low,
crouching posture
used to duck under cars
if I move all of a sudden, but now,
in her tentative way, crawls
into my lap.

Then the thwack of a bat on TV
makes us jump. The sky blazes white,
the inside of my eyelids
are roiling white. That sweet moment
before impact, don't waste it.

Sober Laundry

My clothes are eaten by suds,
bolted door on the washer
like the portal of a ship,
thick glass showing the world's
sea level rising—I'm buoyant,
on my way. I can swing
bags of laundry, heave the anvil
of detergent, but on the other side
of this sea, someone I love
can't lift the battery
that powers her heart.

The women who work here
keep plants by the sink.
A cactus angles up
toward the skylight,
and I find a seat in a shaft
of sun.
I want to be alert,
when someone
sights land.

The List

You found out today,
you're finally on The List.
Your email arrives
as I'm watching a movie; Sean Penn
in bed, listless and pale,
oxygen tank crouched close,
tubes threading to his nose—then
the beeper goes off,
his wife throws back the covers,
they hustle to the hospital
where a donor's heart throbs
in the shock of air and next scene,
he emerges, chest stitched
like an alligator purse,
striding down a boardwalk,
daring the wind to slow
his step.

Your mother is still awake,
so we write,
instead of talk about
your big news, hiding our love
like teenage girls—
for obvious reasons, you say;
pump whirring in your chest,
seconds ticking
as she changes the battery
tethered to your body.

Finally, I write back,
you're almost there,
and I don't see you striding
on a boardwalk like Sean Penn,
but climbing stairs to our room
in your athletic way,
credits streaming.

This Is It

Your sternum,
where I rested my head those years
we shared a bed,
has been cracked like a lobster claw,
and a jigsaw in the surgeon's hand
flicks its razor tongue—
Behold the pericardium,
milky veil that guards
your fist of a heart,
finally loosening its grip.

This morning
in a southern state saturated
in sunshine and free
of helmet laws, a young man
was mangled beyond repair,
but his strong heart hunkered down
in its cave, was gently pried out
like a barnacle
and his gift, in its yellow
cushion of fat, was packed in ice,
flown north
and rolled with expert haste
to the West Side of Manhattan
where you sat up in bed dialing
the call that buzzed
in my backpack—you text me,
too: *This is it*,

and by nightfall, surgeons stitch
the pulsing muscle of a stranger
into the cavity of your chest,
atrium to atrium, vein to vein,
and your blood finds
its new hub, and passes
through.

Frankenstein, My Love

I'm surprised you're such a fan
of that cable series and its male lead,
the 19th-century doctor
who brings creatures to life,
a jolt of electricity
jerking their limbs.

You died twice on the table,
you like to say,
getting your ruined heart switched out
for a good one. Your father,
gone since last winter,
was holding up his hand, as if
blocking you:
Not yet. Not yet.

And so you rose, instead,
in a beautiful, salvaged form,
and something passed
between us—new life—
and we made our impossible plans.

NIGHT

Thoughts hatch, soar, crash.
Debris streaks across
the night sky.

I lie in a field of embers.

The alarm says, 3:23.
3:24. 3:25.

Memories have a half-life.
They decay in the crush of new data.

I say your name, and the names of my sister,
grandmother, father.

They cheer me in familiar voices.
I am an early human,
at the mercy of a bumbling,
bicameral brain,
one side calling to the other.

I tell my feet to relax,
tell my calves,
thighs,
hands
to let go their fight.

My cave warms.
I sleep.

IV.

A Space Carved Clean

Light

Circles of shade overlap,
dark crescents
on the park's great concave lawn,
giant green bowl
where dogs leap and clamp their jaws
on Frisbees descending
in slow arcs,
flinging spit.

Trees stake down the scene.
Beneath the wide, paved path,
beneath the stream of bikers
and beat of runners,
beneath strollers and their heavy,
beloved fruit,
tree roots, cool as marble,
mirror their counterpart
above ground,
and our buried selves
stir toward light.

Promise

It finally cracked in half,
your small gift,
a pendant carved with dolphins
that I tied to my backpack.

I'm sitting with the pieces in my lap,
watching birds huddle on a ledge
across the street
and thinking about falcons,
how they snub the Hudson's corrosive
bass and sturgeon,
seizing pigeons instead, mid-flight
over Manhattan.

Wind combs the orange sky.
Clouds lose their silver, and fill with gray.
Prometer poco, entregar mucho,
you wrote when we were courting,
and I repeat the words in English:
Promise little, deliver much,
sending them out into the night.

Even here, above the street,
clots of pollen swoop and shatter,
effervescent,
before they vanish.

Even Now, I Look For You

Some lanky, middle-aged tomboy
stands with dignified resignation
at the pole on a crowded train
and when she turns around,
my eyes search the cloudy,
linoleum floor,
with its red and black flecks,
a river that ferries us
over razored tracks.

Green

Two men rolled out Astroturf
from the giant, horizontal roll
and threaded it under a blade.
I opened the bundle on my balcony
and sat holding the green pelt
in my lap, cutting it to fit.

Now if I blur my eyes,
it looks plush,
and when the sun is parallel
to my building,
the railing casts a shadow
that scores the green
with crisp black lines.

I have found my perimeter
and it is perfect.
I am elevated, but grounded,
reclining in the bouncy mesh
of a deck chair,

using my distant vision for a change,
tin flashing and aluminum paint
on rooftops winking
all the way to Prospect Park,
where trees have fattened,
and one church spire,
parental as a lighthouse,
punctuates the horizon.

What My Neighbors Taught Me

I stretched across my bed,
lights out, windows open.
It was early evening, the air cool.
Neighbors grilled on their balconies
and called to each other,
like people on small boats drifting
in the night.
Their voices wound through
my apartment,
leaving a trail of jokes and easy
innuendo,
and I began to see my life
as someone you wake to,
in a marriage that was once good,
in a place you once loved.

Moving On

In midtown, an articulated bus,
two long cars accordion-hinged,
cuts the corner too sharp,
rear car sweeping
across the sidewalk
and I hop backwards, up onto
the curb,
clumsy with my load,
a comforter packed tight
in plastic,
feathers sharp as pine needles
behind a barn I left behind,
its basement holding a tree trunk
deep in sawdust,
flat top crisscrossed
with the signature of an axe,
windy loft releasing a dark cloud
of bats that circled the pond,
their soft whir found nowhere
in this city carved tight
as an engine,
tonnage of commerce
shifting gears,
reminding me to yield,
and move on.

Mars

It wasn't always
a cold place.

The planet's iron core
sends waves that permeate
its red crust
and shimmer with heat.

Storms rage
for hundreds of years.

Tubes of dust,
miles high, collapse
and snap back up
to their full, undulating
height,
whipping across
the landscape.

I miss you,
at the oddest times.

Pinkish Hue

> *The term "butch" tends to denote a degree of masculinity ... beyond what would be considered typical of a tomboy.*
> 　　--Wikipedia, "Butch-Femme"

It's like that scene in *Seinfeld*,
Jerry setting George up
on a blind date,
and George asks,
What about her hair?
If I stick my hand
in her hair,
can I get my hand out?
Jerry says, *Of course*
you can get your hand out!—
but George isn't satisfied.
Does she have
a pinkish hue?
Her cheek? I like a cheek
with a pinkish hue.

I am George.
Does she have a closet of button-down
shirts? She has to have a closet
of button-down shirts.

Dinner Date

Before we moved to my bed,
we sat in separate chairs with glasses
of wine. I handed her the phone
and she whisked through
my vacation photos,
stopped on a pink cactus splayed
against stucco,
and with her thumb
and forefinger,
snapped the image open,
revealed the lavender tongue,
glided her finger to telescope
the nodding, spiky bloom,
taking her time.

After Hearing Your Message

I'm a kid caught with answers
scribbled on my wrist.
I'm a stray cat spotting a can of tuna
on the stoop.
I'm a woman driving across
the Brooklyn Bridge at sunset,
sky a wall of flames that darkens
as I descend,
one silver cloud torn apart by fish,
in the lavender sky.

Lunch, After Time Apart

My sandals slap down three flights
to the train platform.
"Wet Paint" signs flutter
and the reek of turpentine is buoyed
by heat. We're meeting
in a Thai restaurant,
and its cool dark calms me as I wait.
Beads clatter at your arrival.
Our conversation skips and stalls
and then—*We want the same things*,
you say, and my relief rains down
in a tepid wash. Leaving,
we gather the small white boxes,
step from Arctic air
to the surface of the sun.
Heat swims above the sidewalk.
Silver flashes along your temple.
I put my hand on your back,
brush over wings tucked sharp
beneath your scorched shirt.
You are my falcon;
you dropped fish at my feet.
You tore back my skin,
like the lid of a can.
I smooth your collar,
while we stand talking.

The Usefulness of Storms

Lightning strikes
eight million times a day.

Deflect the bolt,
and you amplify
its power.

Absorb
the ion surge,
and you become
its vessel.

The only safe place
is beneath a cloudless sky,

but I love precipitation.
Veins of light zigzag
through clouds ripe
as plums.

Look what we made,
I say to the storm
as it melts away,

and the din of insects
claims a space
carved clean.

V.

BURNT SCENT RISING

Discovery

Two jets hit the Towers and fuel exploded,
chunks of metal shot like shrapnel
over Lower Manhattan,
one piece plummeting between two buildings,
missing the roof on either side,
where it would have sunk like a hot brick
in snow.

Surveyors found that fist of steel
a decade later,
wedged into a narrow space I pass
each morning,
walking to work,
the Medical Examiner's
white awning blocking the sidewalk,
the City renewing its search
for human remains.

Workers sifted through sediment
for splinters of bone, the shard of a tooth.
For weeks they conducted
their delicate excavation,
as if the detritus of loss can be named
and reassembled,
as if there is good in that.

Hawai'i

My sister and I were taught,
if a shark glided toward us,
to make a fist and punch
that slick, blunt snout,
bluffing for our lives,
causing the small, dim eyes
to shift robotically
beyond us.
We had superhuman strength.
We had white limbs that fluttered
in cloudy water.

Sparks

I raked the burn pile
in the woods behind a house
I lived in once,
and found a doll,
eyes rattling, skull heavy
with dirt,
plastic body singed.
My sister was still here:
From action to object to symbol,
we articulate creation,
she wrote in a poem I found
on her hard drive
and I add for her today,
Then we erase
what we have made.
A lover slept beside me,
then. Sparks flashed
from the blanket,
every time she turned.

Hers

My small lawn floats
a dozen stories above the street.
If I lie flat on a yoga mat,
wind kicks over me
like the back legs of cattle our corgi
chased that summer
on our grandparents' farm,
my sister and I, with our new,
surprising breasts, wandering the pasture
in T-strap sandals
and naming all the cows.

Today is her birthday, and mine
comes soon after.
When we were small,
she taunted me
those few days our age aligned,
and now fourteen years divide us.

Afternoon sun bakes the balcony's
fake grass carpet.
I move to one of two red chairs
and adjust the hat I bought
for some vacation; Provincetown
or California, wide brim
and mesh crown, not really
my style,
so much as hers.

Biking at the End of Summer

My heart is punching
my ribs,
burnt scent rising
from tar-patched pot holes
along my route.
I'm skimming a plateau dappled
with shadow.
Three women in sundresses
are pushing strollers,
and striding beside them,
a young man maneuvers
a cart that holds a cooler,
solemn about his task as Bill Paxton's
character, the Mormon husband
in *Big Love*, sister wives chatting
in the kitchen.

Later I take a shower,
and in the wrap of steam,
wave my arms slowly,
water sloshing
against the deep sides of a tub,
my young father expertly gripping
my heel, scrubbing
the small sole darkened
by playing outside in bare feet,
relishing his task.

We Climb to an Empty Roof

At night we wrap ourselves
in wool,
the stitched hides of animals
whose ghosts flicker
like airplane lights.
We climb to an empty roof.
The sky is busy as a river,
we dream of swimming.

VI.
BEVELED EDGE SHINING

Comfort Food

There is talk of *comfort food*,
but all food
comforts me. Toast
comforts me. Rice pudding
comforts me. A rotisserie chicken,
glowing like a sacrifice
in the refrigerator's scalding
white mouth, comforts me.

Dog

It's late but I'm rinsing kale,
sliding my thumb down the flat white spine
to loosen anything left
of the garden.
I miss you the most at night,
and lying in bed, repeat some inane phrase:
Everything's great, counting
on fingertips smooth as rosary beads.

When the weather warms,
I sit outside.
A neighbor's white bull terrier
shakes his collar on the balcony
next to mine, sniffs the potted flowers
and pushes his big head
through railing.
He stares down at the street,
wagging his blunt tail.
He pulls his head back in,
regards me intently
with tiny, pink eyes,
and I see myself as he does,
just another human
sitting outside, floating
in a chair, a resolute red chair.

Nest

Driving home, I listened to sanitation
workers on NPR,
and one old timer whose brother, nephew
and cousins all made a living
collecting garbage—
and both my daughters
have master's degrees,
he announced as I reached my garage,
entrance blocked by a garbage truck,
it turns out,

so I sat regarding the two men
in their orange vests,
leisurely swinging bags
into the compactor's foul mouth,
pausing to gesture mildly
in a conversation that floated
above their task,

their truck also blocking a man
and his tiny daughter
on the sidewalk beside my car.
Look, he told her, pointing
to the building's eave.
Look up, right there. See the baby
bird? See the mama
and her baby? and when the child
in her white dress and diaphanous
cloud of hair didn't see,

he lifted her high in front of him,
brandished her up toward heaven
as if bragging to the gods,
and the garbage truck flattened
its last bite with an agonizing
screech, and she saw.

Mother, Sister, Friend

Some who loved you
still resent that you smoked,
inhaling nicotine that frayed
your veins.
Residue burrowed
in the coral of your brain.
Smoke followed you
down a hallway,
hovered as you hooked
a string of cowbells
to your four-year-old's
bedroom doorknob,
a child who made nighttime
escapes and stood wielding
a shard of glass
as I pulled into your driveway
in a rented car.
I understand now,
how the cigarette raised
your energy a degree or two,
when you drifted
just over zero.
It waited every dark place
you put your hand.

Flight

There are two kinds of people—those afraid
of heights, and those who imagine
jumping. I know
which type I am. All my life, I watched
my father lift off, coast and land,
a young man in a flight suit rippling
with zippers, an old man
with white hair, sipping coffee
in a cockpit, horizon
a blistering red line. Dying now
in an oxygen mask, he stands,
a small boy on the edge
of a cliff, surveying the vast,
confusing light.
He fills his lungs,
capillaries pulse like strings
of lights. He calculates the speed
of his own weight
falling, and stretches out his arms.
I take his hand. We leap.

Sober Cooking

The vegetables are blue-black, ruby,
white. I strop the knife blade
on a whetstone, the whisking sound
fast, the beveled edge shining
to another degree
of thinness.

My father liked to call
when I was cooking for the week,
and he wanted to hear
ingredients: ginger, turmeric,
quinoa; their origin
continents away
from the sweet rolls and bacon
we devoured as a young family
in a string of small houses linked,
for me, by falling asleep
to the muffled drone
of a black-and-white TV
in another room,
my parents talking quietly
over the tinny laugh track,
their shoes kicked off,
legs stretched out
on an ottoman.

I remember sleepwalking, too,
waking in front of that TV,
and my parents' solicitous voices
as they knelt before me,
my hand locked on the channel knob,
static crackling
a few inches from my face.

It's the kind of thing I think of,
when I'm sharpening a knife
on the thick,
rectangular stone my grandmother
gave me, and her grandmother
gave her. It's the kind of thing
I remember when I'm sober,
cooking.

Killing Time at the Cubbyhole

The ceiling is the ocean's floor, turned
upside down,
strands of Christmas garland
and fake flowers swirling thick
as seaweed.

The bartender has a bouquet tattooed
on her neck, and hands me
a glass of wine. I back my stool
into a corner,
sternum vibrating with the speakers'
thumping bass.

A man rushes up from the basement,
dumps a bucket of ice
behind the bar, and I'm a teenager
on my father's boat,
grouper freezing
in the hull as we slap across
the waves.
He's got the steering wheel
in one hand, cold beer
in the other, sun making
our faces amber.

A woman stands in front of me,
waiting for her drink,
back of her fur vest bristling
against my knees.

Celine Dion belts out the theme song
to *The Titanic* and I'm in Ecuador
with a lover, the one who rolled her eyes
as musicians in ponchos
brandished wooden flutes, exhaling
the same American hits
in every town,
flocks of parrots painting
the sky.

People I've loved shimmer
like holograms, diffuse like snow.
I'm on another glass of wine, watching
someone carry a couple cocktails back
to her table. She pivots
through the crowd,
and over her head, a touchdown
is repeating itself,
players in red uniforms
throwing big arms across
each other's shoulders, dancing
in a tight ring,
like cherubs.

The Dead Visit Before a Routine Procedure

I fanned out, light as a leaf,
elixir darkening my veins.
A nurse grounded me
with a blanket hot from the dryer,
and I waited in a cube
marked off by curtains;
time, an oven door cracked open
and my father, sister and grandmother
gathered in the wavy air
with their gentle, long faces
and pale eyes.
An attendant
with a merman's wet, black curls
rolled me down a hallway,
under a fluorescent keyboard—
dark, light, dark, light, dark—
and I was stored somewhere safe.
Then a nurse was standing
by my bed, offering
apple juice and crackers,
and I was back
in the world of teeth
and trains, the world I hate
and love.

Urban Renewal

The steaming core of the City
seeps through
sidewalk grates,
intimate and warm
as a caged animal's
breath.
I step on soft tar,
I am almost home.

Acknowledgements

American Poetry Review: "Hawaii"

Big City Lit: "The Dead Visit Before a Routine Procedure"

Right Hand Pointing: "Urban Renewal"

Storyscape: "I Leave You Listed," "Scar" and "Small Flame" (as "Second Round")

NOTES

Biking at the End of Summer: *Big Love* is a fictional drama series that aired on HBO from 2006 to 2011 and featured a polygamist Mormon family and its patriarch played by Bill Paxton.

Daily Life: In August 2013 in Bay Ridge, Brooklyn, ice cream truck driver Mina Gatas was busted in an investigation dubbed "Operation: Snowcone" and accused of selling narcotics from his truck.

Frankenstein, My Love: The drama series *Penny Dreadful,* which first aired on Showtime in 2014, employs 19th-century characters from British horror fiction.

Killing Time at the Cubbyhole: The Cubbyhole is a lesbian bar in the West Village of New York City.

Our First ER and **ER**: "ER" stands for "Emergency Room," though hospitals are shifting now to "Emergency Department."

Pinkish Hue: *Seinfeld* is a television sitcom that originally aired on NBC from 1989 to 1998. The character George Costanza was played by Jason Alexander.

Pocket of Life: Sauropods were the dominant herbivore dinosaurs of the Jurassic Period, weighing over 100 tons and characterized by their long necks and tails.

Prey: The 1959 Alfred Hitchcock movie in which Cary Grant is chased by a crop duster is *North by Northwest*.

Promise: Since 1983, state and federal agencies as well as organizations such as The Peregrine Fund have provided nesting boxes and released falcons in New York City where they thrive on pigeons and other animals, avoiding the pesticide-laced fish in the Hudson River that were causing their eggs to break before maturation.

The In-between: *The Sopranos* is a crime drama series that first aired on HBO from 1999 through 2007 and centers on the character Tony Soprano, played by the late James Gandolfini.

The List: In the 2013 movie *21 Grams*, Sean Penn plays a character that undergoes a heart transplant.

Written in the Sky: Certain lines in this poem parody a 1990s advertising campaign for the international chemical producer BASF.

LYNN MCGEE has won two chapbook contests: *Bonanza* was published by Slapering Hol Press of the Hudson Valley Writers Center in 1997 and *Heirloom Bulldog* was published by Bright Hill Press in 2015. *Sober Cooking*, from Spuyten Duyvil Press, is her first full-length collection. Her poems have appeared in many journals, including *The American Poetry Review, Southern Poetry Review, Ontario Review, Hawai'i Review, Storyscape, 2 Bridges Review, Painted Bride Quarterly, The Same, Sun Magazine, Phoebe, Laurel Review* and *The New Guard*; one poem a finalist and one a semi-finalist in the Knightville contest judged by Donald Hall. She earned an MFA in Poetry at Columbia University, was awarded a MacDowell fellowship, is a winner of the Judith's Room Award, and taught freshman writing at private and public universities as well as having led poetry workshops in public schools. She is a recipient of the NYC Literacy Assistance Center's Recognition Award for her work in adult literacy, and received the Heart of the Center Award from the LGBT Community Center in New York City for developing, as a volunteer, their first GED class. Today she is a staff writer at Borough of Manhattan Community College, City University of New York and co-curates, with Gerry LaFemina, the Lunar Walk Poetry Series in Brooklyn, New York.